Autumn

I Love You This Much, Nonna

Written by
JAMES DOTI

Illustrated by
BAGRAM IBATOULLINE

Dear Reader,

As I think far back in time, it's as if I'm looking into a window and see a memory — a memory of my grandmother. I see her standing next to our Christmas tree, smiling at me and my little dog, Blackie.

I call her "Nonna."

Christmas is Nonna's favorite holiday. She especially loves the sparkling lights and shimmering ornaments on the tree.

In that Christmas memory, we are waiting for my parents to wake up so we can open our presents. We munch on the biscotti di cannella that I helped Nonna bake. The cookies' spicy cinnamon smell mingles nicely with the earthy pine scent of the tree.

In an excited voice, I ask, "Can I open one present, Nonna? Just one?"

Eagerly tearing away at the brightly wrapped present Nonna hands me, I find inside a red and white sweater that she knitted.

"I love it, Nonna!" I shout, pulling it on over my head and circling around so she can see it fits perfectly. Then Nonna grabs and kisses me.

In the story to follow, you'll discover that Nonna and I are "kindred spirits." That means we share a special bond, because we like being with each other and doing fun things together.

This story is also about losing and finding someone you love.

Your friend, Jimmy

Summer

When Nonna visits Jimmy in the summer, they walk almost every day to a beautiful park in the middle of the city. A sign at the entrance is anchored by two stone columns and reads, "Portage Park."

Their favorite spot is a bench facing a fountain where robins and sparrows come to drink and bathe. Jimmy and Nonna laugh as they toss out cookie crumbs and watch the birds fight over them. Blackie is so transfixed watching the birds that he doesn't bark at them—not even once.

When the crumbs are gone, Jimmy says excitedly, "Dad got me a new comic book!" Jimmy likes reading to Nonna, especially stories about cowboys. Nonna listens intently while Jimmy reads aloud. Her eyes probe the sky, as if she can see a cowboy riding through the clouds.

As they leave the park, Nonna, Jimmy and Blackie walk slowly. The afternoon sun beats down on them. Approaching Connie's Italian Ice push cart, Jimmy asks, "Can I have a lemon ice for Nonna, a chocolate one for me and a cup of water for Blackie?"

Jimmy and Nonna enjoy their Italian ices. They laugh at seeing Blackie hold onto his cup and quickly slurp the water.

Pop! Pop! Pop!

The July 4th fireworks light the nighttime sky over Nonna and Jimmy's heads. They see sparkles of light explode sharply and then slowly fizzle away to nothing.

Nonna is staying with Jimmy while his mom and dad are away for the holiday. Blackie is in the house curled up in a tight ball under Jimmy's bed. The loud pops of the fireworks scare him.

"Can we light the sparklers now? Can we?" Jimmy asks eagerly.

Nonna carefully lights the ends of two sparklers and hands them to Jimmy. He waves the sparklers around, their white trails of light following his movements.

Nonna then starts a little game they love to play together. She holds her hands out in front of her, placing them closely together, and asks, "Do you love me this much?" Jimmy says "No," and Nonna keeps asking her question over and over, making the space between her hands bigger and bigger each time—and Jimmy keeps answering louder and louder, "No!"

"Well, then, how much do you love me?" Nonna asks. That's when Jimmy stretches his arms as wide as he can. With sparks flying at his sides, he laughs loudly while he exclaims, "I love you this much, Nonna!"

Autumn

A gust of chilly wind blows more of the leaves from Portage Park's nearly naked elm trees. Nonna tells Jimmy that it's a sign of good luck to catch a falling leaf. So he runs quickly, arms outstretched, trying to catch the leaves as they flutter through the air like butterflies.

A lone robin perched on the fountain keeps a keen eye on Blackie; then flies away.

"Why are all the robins flying away?" Jimmy asks.

"They'll be back in the spring," Nonna answers.

"But why do they leave?"

"That's just the way it is, Jimmy. They fly away, but I promise you that they will fly back."

Jimmy notices that Nonna seems frail as she struggles to get up from the bench to go home.

For every Thanksgiving that Jimmy can remember, Nonna comes to visit. The family would be wakened early by the sounds of Nonna bustling around the kitchen, making ravioli, adding her tasty Italian sausage stuffing to the turkey, and baking her special cookies—biscotti di cannella.

But when Jimmy wakes up this Thanksgiving morning, the house is quiet. Nonna is nowhere to be seen.

"Nonna is still in bed," Jimmy's mom says. "She's not feeling well, but she wants to see you and Blackie."

Entering the bedroom, Jimmy sees Nonna bundled under thick covers. Her skin is pale and her smile is weak, not the vibrant smile Jimmy is used to seeing.

Blackie stays close to Jimmy's side. Blackie's tail, which always wags briskly when he sees Nonna, is still.

Jimmy can see that Nonna is too frail to play their favorite game, so he decides to improvise. He holds out his arms with his hands very close to each other and says, "I don't love you this much." He spreads his hands out a little more and says, "I don't love you even this much." Then, moving his arms apart as wide as he can, he tells her loudly, "I love you this much, Nonna!"

Though Nonna doesn't say anything, she smiles and pulls her hand out from under the covers to give Jimmy's hand a gentle squeeze.

The following Monday afternoon, Jimmy walks out the doors of Reinberg School. His mom is parked at the side of the road. Even from a distance, he can see a sad look on her face.

Before his mom can say anything, Jimmy knows why she's there. It's about Nonna.

As his mom turns and faces him, Jimmy sees tears come to her eyes. Then, in a calm, soft voice, she says, "I have very sad news, Jimmy. Nonna passed away this morning."

Jimmy doesn't say anything.

His mom doesn't say anything either, but she hugs Jimmy tightly as they cry in each other's arms.

The week after Nonna's funeral, Jimmy is lying on his bed with Blackie nuzzling at his feet. Jimmy is wearing the red and white sweater that Nonna knitted for him. He stares at the framed photo on his bedside table and realizes how much he misses her.

Jimmy goes to his desk and takes his crayons and paper out of the drawer. Then he sits down and starts to draw something he knows Nonna would like.

When he's done, Jimmy places the drawing next to the framed photo of Nonna.

Winter

The park is silent, somber, buried in new-fallen snow. Nothing seems alive anymore.

Jimmy knows what it means to die. Just a few weeks ago, he saw his friend Mary Ambrose sitting alone and crying during recess. When he asked her what was wrong, she told him that her cat, Tabitha, had died.

But until Nonna died, death had never happened so close to Jimmy.

Now, looking out from the bench where he and Blackie and Nonna used to sit happily together, Jimmy sees gnarled crystal icicles around the frozen fountain. No birds are there to dunk themselves in the water. Nonna isn't there to listen to Jimmy read comic books.

It's just Blackie and him sitting alone, shivering together on a cold, icy bench.

Later that evening, Jimmy's dad tells him, "It's a family tradition that there is a period of mourning when someone very close to us, like Nonna, passes away." He pauses and then says, "That means, out of respect and love for Nonna, we won't have a Christmas tree or decorations this year."

Jimmy thinks about that for a moment, but it doesn't make any sense to him. "Nonna would want us to have a tree," he tells his dad. "She loved Christmas trees and all the decorations."

"No, Jimmy, it's not the right thing to do," his dad answers. "We must follow our family's tradition."

Two days before Christmas, Jimmy and his dad take Blackie out for a walk. But Blackie doesn't like the cold, crusty snow, so he rides on a sled that Jimmy pulls behind him.

Jimmy looks at the Christmas trees sparkling in the windows of the homes they pass. He remembers how Nonna's face glowed whenever she saw a brightly lit Christmas tree.

Turning a corner, Jimmy and his dad walk by a familiar sign that reads "Dominic's Christmas Trees—Best in Town!" Then Jimmy sees it—one tree, tied up with string and leaning against the side of a small shed. He stops and shouts out, "Dad, let's buy that tree and bring it home to surprise Mom."

Dominic stands by a fire, warming his hands over the flames. Hearing Jimmy's idea, he says, "Since that's my last tree, I can sell it to you for two bucks. If you buy it, we can all go home. Haw Haw."

Before Jimmy's dad can say "No," Dominic plops the tree on the sled, right next to Blackie.

Arriving home, they start up the stairway that leads to the door of their second-floor apartment. Jimmy follows behind his dad, who slowly pulls the tree up, one step at a time.

The turn between the two flights of stairs is very narrow. Jimmy's dad pulls and pulls but can't get the tree around the corner. It's stuck on the handrail and just won't budge. Getting down on his knees, Jimmy's dad pulls with all the force he can muster. Suddenly, the tip of the tree swings forward like a slingshot and knocks him over. Struggling to get up, he hollers, "Why'd we ever get this darn tree?"

Jimmy runs to his dad, puts his arms around him and pleads, "No, no, Daddy! It's a nice tree."

Feeling the tight grip of arms around him, Jimmy's dad looks down at his little boy with bewilderment. He can't quite figure out how Jimmy convinced him to break a family tradition by getting a Christmas tree during a time of mourning.

Leaving a trail of pine needles on their path to the living room, Jimmy and his dad untie the strings wrapped tightly around the tree. The tree's branches spring open and reveal a startling surprise. Only a few needles are left!

Just then, Jimmy's mom walks into the living room and sees the almost bare tree leaning against the wall.

"Oh, what a beautiful Christmas tree!" she exclaims.

Jimmy and his dad gape at her in amazement, wondering what she sees that they don't.

Jimmy's mom carts boxes of Christmas lights and ornaments from the basement storage. Then she goes to work on the barren tree. After she is done stringing multicolored lights around the tree, Jimmy helps hang the ornaments. He decorates the lower branches, while his mom decorates the higher ones.

As the tree is transformed into something wonderful, Blackie excitedly runs around it, his tail wagging briskly.

Jimmy's mom sees one last ornament wrapped in old newspaper. She removes the paper with great care and says in a soft voice that is almost a whisper, "Ah… here it is… Nonna's ornament." She holds out an angel that looks like a little girl with wings.

Jimmy knows that Nonna brought the angel with her from Brienza, the village in Italy where she grew up. Every Christmas, when she hung her treasured ornament on the tree, Nonna would tell Jimmy a story of her early life there.

As Jimmy's dad takes the precious angel into his hands, Jimmy searches his father's face in hopes of seeing his approval of the new tree.

Tenderly cradling the angel, Jimmy's father turns to him with a gentle smile and says, "You were right, Jimmy. Nonna would have wanted us to have a Christmas tree, and I know she would have loved this one."

Spring

Just as Nonna promised, the robins return in the spring. They frolic with the sparrows in the fountain's watery spray. Red and purple tulips show off their beauty along Portage Park's pathways. Tightly folded elm leaves not yet ready to open look like millions of green dots speckling the trees.

Jimmy and Blackie are at their usual bench. Although the nippy winter chill is gone, Nonna's red and white sweater keeps Jimmy warm in the crisp morning air.

Jimmy smiles as memories of Nonna flood his mind. He thinks about how much they loved watching fireworks, laughing at the birds fighting over cookie crumbs, reading comic books and having Italian ice on a hot, muggy day.

Ever since Christmas, when his dad placed Nonna's ornament on their very special tree, Jimmy's sad thoughts about Nonna's death have slowly given way to happy memories of the fun they had together. He realizes that Nonna isn't really gone. Nonna's soft voice, tender touch and gentle smile will always be there. Nonna, Jimmy now knows, lives inside him.

Jimmy pulls Blackie up on the bench. Raising Blackie's two front paws, Jimmy asks, "Do you love me this much?" Spreading Blackie's paws out wider, Jimmy asks, "Blackie, I bet you love me this much, don't you!"

Blackie looks puzzled as Jimmy laughs and laughs.

From Jimmy to You

It's been more than sixty years since Nonna died. Despite the passing of all those years, hardly a day has gone by that I haven't thought of her.

Even now, as I help my two grandsons, Parker and Griffin, make biscotti di cannella, I tell them stories about Nonna. And while it wasn't funny when it happened, they laugh when they hear about their great-grandpa getting hit in the face by that very special Christmas tree.

Parker adds the cinnamon to the cookie dough, while Griffin adds walnuts.

Taking a tray of steaming cookies out of the oven, several fall on the floor and break into pieces. Parker picks them up and walks to the trash to throw them away.

I stop him and say, "Let's walk to the park and feed those crumbs to the birds."

Hearing me say the word "walk," my dog, Angel, twirls around and around in circles, tail wagging briskly, just like Blackie used to do.

Nonna's Biscotti di Cannella

½ cup unsalted butter at room temperature
    (If using salted butter, omit the salt indicated below.)
1 cup sugar
1 large egg
1 teaspoon vanilla
1-½ cups flour
1 teaspoon cinnamon
1 teaspoon baking powder
¼ teaspoon salt
½ cup walnut pieces (optional but they make the cookies yummy)
Red and green sugar sprinkles

Preheat oven at 350°

Cream together butter and sugar with a mixer. Then beat in egg and vanilla.

Combine flour, cinnamon, baking powder, salt and walnuts in a separate bowl.

Add flour mixture to sugar-butter mixture and mix until it comes together in the form of cookie dough.

Cover cookie dough and refrigerate one hour.

Shape refrigerated dough into small balls about an inch in diameter and place them about one inch apart on greased cookie sheet.

Bake for 10 minutes. (Don't worry if cookies appear soft. They will harden as they cool.)

As soon as cookies are removed from the oven, top with red and green sugar sprinkles.

Allow sprinkled cookies to cool on a rack.

Then find a cozy place where you can eat them while reading a favorite book.

Enjoy!

For my grandsons, Parker James and Griffin Thomas,
who love to make biscotti di cannella.

– J.D.

For my dear grandparents.

– B.I.

fern-press.com
fernpressinfo@gmail.com

ISBN - 978-0-692-19664-9

Editorial and Design Assistance by Ann Cameron

Printed in the United States of America

Winter